Blue Banner Biography

John Legend

Bonnie Hinman

Mitchell Lane
PUBLISHERS

P.O. Box 196
Hockessin, Delaware 19707
Visit us on the web: www.mitchelllane.com
Comments? email us: mitchelllane@mitchelllane.com

Mitchell Lane

Printing   1   2   3   4   5   6   7   8   9

Blue Banner Biographies

Akon	Alan Jackson	Alicia Keys
Allen Iverson	Ashanti	Ashlee Simpson
Ashton Kutcher	Avril Lavigne	Bernie Mac
Beyoncé	Bow Wow	Brett Favre
Britney Spears	Carrie Underwood	Chris Brown
Chris Daughtry	Christina Aguilera	Christopher Paul Curtis
Ciara	Clay Aiken	Cole Hamels
Condoleezza Rice	Corbin Bleu	Daniel Radcliffe
David Ortiz	Derek Jeter	Eminem
Eve	Fergie (Stacy Ferguson)	50 Cent
Gwen Stefani	Ice Cube	Jamie Foxx
Jay-Z	Jennifer Lopez	Ja Rule
J.K. Rowling	John Legend	Jessica Simpson
Joe Flacco	Johnny Depp	JoJo
Justin Berfield	Justin Timberlake	Kanye West
Kate Hudson	Keith Urban	Kelly Clarkson
Kenny Chesney	Kristen Stewart	Lance Armstrong
Leona Lewis	Lil Wayne	Lindsay Lohan
Mariah Carey	Mario	Mary J. Blige
Mary-Kate and Ashley Olsen	Miguel Tejada	Missy Elliott
Nancy Pelosi	Natasha Bedingfield	Nelly
Orlando Bloom	P. Diddy	Paris Hilton
Peyton Manning	Pink	Queen Latifah
Rihanna	Ron Howard	Rudy Giuliani
Sally Field	Sean Kingston	Selena
Shakira	Shontelle Layne	Soulja Boy Tell 'Em
Taylor Swift	T.I.	Timbaland
Tim McGraw	Toby Keith	Usher
Vanessa Anne Hudgens	Zac Efron	

Library of Congress Cataloging-in-Publication Data
Hinman, Bonnie.
  John Legend / by Bonnie Hinman.
    p. cm. — (Blue banner biographies)
  Includes bibliographical references and index.
  ISBN 978-1-58415-774-8 (library bound : alk. paper)
  1. Legend, John — Juvenile literature. 2. Rhythm and blues musicians — United States — Biography — Juvenile literature. I. Title.
  ML3930.L33H56 2009
  782.421644092 — dc22
  [B]
                                                                          2009006308

ABOUT THE AUTHOR: Bonnie Hinman loves music and singing and enjoys learning more about modern soul music, including rap and hip-hop. A graduate of Missouri State University, she is the author of twenty books for young readers, including *Extreme Cycling with Dale Holmes* for Mitchell Lane Publishers. She lives in Southwest Missouri with her husband, Bill, near her children and four grandchildren.

Blue Banner Biography

John Legend opened the half-time show for the 2009 NBA All-Star Game in Phoenix, Arizona, on February 15. He performed an extended version of "If You're Out There," a single from his Evolver *album. Legend first performed the song at the 2008 Democratic Convention and considers its message as a call to action on behalf of responsibility, leadership, and commitment to a better tomorrow.*

Music Prodigy

*H*allelujah" was the first thing John Legend's mother said when he called to tell her he had been nominated for eight Grammy awards. She had a right to be excited that her twenty-seven-year-old son had been so honored. Only stars Mariah Carey and Kanye West had received so many nominations for the important music awards for 2005. It was even sweeter because this was the first year that John had been in the running. His first studio album, *Get Lifted*, had debuted at the end of December 2004.

Legend later told *USA Today* of his eight nominations, "I was floored. I couldn't believe it." The Grammy show aired on February 13, 2006. John was asked to sing his hit single, "Ordinary People," as part of the entertainment. One of the highlights for him happened during rehearsal when Paul McCartney of the Beatles approached the piano where John was playing. A few weeks later, John told *Rolling Stone* interviewer Austin Scaggs, "He walked up to the piano and said, 'Sorry, but I just wanted to tell you that I think your song is beautiful.' Meeting him was cool but getting a compliment from one of the best songwriters in the world was very, very cool."

Unlike many other singers, John writes his own songs and takes songwriting very seriously. "Ordinary People" was nominated for Best Song of the Year, which is a songwriter's award. Legend told an *Orlando Sentinel* reporter, "To get nominated for that is very gratifying."

> **Unlike many other singers, John writes his own songs and takes songwriting very seriously.**

Legend went to the podium three times that night to collect awards. He told Scaggs that he was very nervous when he gave his three thank-you speeches, and he forgot to thank just about everybody. According to Scaggs, Legend later laughed and said, "I forgot to thank so many people that at least they're in good company."

John took home the trophies for Best New Artist, Best R&B (rhythm and blues) Album, and Best Male R&B Vocal Performance for "Ordinary People." It was a nice reward for many months of touring, but only the beginning for the talented young songwriter, singer, and pianist.

John also admitted in the *Rolling Stone* interview, "I'm still floatin' on air." But his feet were actually planted on the ground, because the next thing he said was, "I'm ready to make another album. I'm pumped. I'm ready to do this." He went back to his Manhattan apartment to work on songs for a new album.

John came on the music scene suddenly—or so it seemed. But as often happens, he had been working and preparing for his Grammy awards his entire life. He was born in Springfield, Ohio, on December 28, 1978. His last name was Stephens then, and his family often called him Johnny.

John's father, Ronald Stephens, was a factory worker, and his mother, Phyllis, was a seamstress and homemaker. His childhood centered on the church and music. His mother directed the church choir; his grandmother was the organist; his father and older brother, Ronald II, played drums; and his grandfather was the pastor. When John was four years old, he asked for piano lessons so that he could be a part of the musical fun.

Legend proudly displays two of the three Grammy Awards he won at the 49th annual event on February 12, 2007, in Los Angeles.

His parents agreed even though he couldn't yet reach the pedals on the piano, which sat in their front room. It didn't take long for John's musical talent to blossom. By the time he was six, he was singing in the church choir and playing the piano for services. When he was eleven, he directed the choir.

Legend spoke of the church's influence on his musical career in a 2006 interview with *Newsweek*. "It's such a great training ground for young black musicians. You have an audience, it's an important part of the service and it makes you want to be a better musician."

"I'm ready to make another album. I'm pumped. I'm ready to do this."

John wasn't only a music prodigy. He skipped two grades in elementary school, and won Springfield's city spelling contest when he was in fourth grade. He graduated from North High School at age sixteen, as the school's salutatorian. He considered himself a nerd in school because of his good grades and love of learning, but he was also well liked.

Two more children were added to the family after John. Vaughn came next, and then Missy, the only girl. The family was close then, as they continue to be.

John took part in all the high school music opportunities, including musicals and talent shows. He started two different R&B bands during his teenage years and continued to sing and play at church.

Right after high school, John became a freshman at the University of Pennsylvania. He was young for college, but his love of music helped him fit in and succeed with the older students.

John "the Legend"

At the university, John joined a jazz and pop singing group called Counterparts. They performed a cappella, or without instrumental accompaniment, and received national recognition while John was a member. He was both president and music director for the group. John majored in English with an emphasis on African American literature.

He also worked as a choir director and pianist at the Bethel AME Church in Scranton, Pennsylvania, just outside Philadelphia. He kept this job for nine years. Besides providing money, the church job kept him in touch with his musical roots.

When Stephens was nineteen, a friend invited him to go with her to a recording session with hip-hop star Lauryn Hill. The friend, Tara Michel, was a backup singer for Hill. Tara bragged about John's musical talents until Hill listened to him play the piano. Hill agreed with Tara and hired John to play piano for "Everything Is Everything." The song would later become a hit single from her debut album, *The Miseducation of Lauryn Hill.*

Hill invited Stephens to try out for her band. He was willing to drop out of college to take advantage of this opportunity, but after the audition, he wasn't hired. John talked about his disappointment in a later interview with Joss Stone for *Interview* magazine. "When I was younger I thought I was supposed to have a record deal by age 19 or 20. When it didn't happen, I would get frustrated, but I would keep working and progressing and making new songs and recording new demos."

Legend, along with guitarist Sharief Hobley and singers Jessica Wilson and Tara Michel, performed an in-flight concert to celebrate the 50th anniversary of the Grammys. Fifty lucky music fans won a seat on the Delta Airlines Grammy plane for the trip from New York City to Los Angeles for the Grammy Awards broadcast in 2008.

Instead of going on the road with Hill, John stayed in school and graduated in 1999. He moved to New York City to take a management consulting job with Boston Consulting Group. The new job paid well above what most new college graduates make, but it was a means to an end for him. It allowed him to live comfortably in New York City while he spent his evenings and weekends singing and playing piano in nightclubs from New York to Philadelphia.

John self-produced two albums of his music while he was working the nightclub circuit. They were released under his given name, John Stephens, as *John Stephens* (2000) and *Live at Jimmy's Uptown* (2001). He sold the CDs at his performances and on his web site.

John's biggest break came in 2002 when his roommate and fellow musician, DeVon Harris, introduced him to Kanye West, who was DeVon's cousin. Hip-hop artist West was on the way to success. The two performers became good friends, and each was important in the other's career. They collaborated closely on each other's albums.

West also introduced John to several established artists who hired him to play piano and sing backup vocals. He worked with Janet Jackson, Alicia Keys, Jay-Z, the Black Eyed Peas, and Twista. He also cowrote some songs with Jackson and Keys.

Chicago poet J. Ivy was at one of the recording sessions for West's album, *The College Dropout*, and heard Stephens sing. He called John "the Legend" because he sounded so

> *"When I was younger I thought I was supposed to have a record deal by age 19 or 20. When it didn't happen, I would get frustrated..."*

much like soul singers of the past, including Stevie Wonder and Marvin Gaye. The nickname stuck, and eventually John Stephens became John Legend.

After the success of *The College Dropout*, West started his own record label, G.O.O.D. (Getting Out Our Dreams) under Sony/BMG. The first artist he signed was John Legend. West was the executive producer of what would become Legend's award-winning album, *Get Lifted*.

> *John's biggest break came in 2002 when his roommate and fellow musician, DeVon Harris, introduced him to Kanye West.*

When interviewed by *People* magazine in March 2005, Legend said that West "has great instincts. He gives me a lot of good advice on the creative level. We critique each other's song productions. He also gives me good advice on dealing with the record industry."

After *Get Lifted* was finished but not yet released, Legend opened for West on West's 2004 tour. One song was released before the album. "Used to Love U" eventually peaked at number 32 on the Hot R&B/Hip-Hop Singles & Tracks chart. Legend also did a small-venue and college tour in December 2004 to build excitement for the album. The excitement was building—but releasing an album is only the beginning of the hard work required to sell it.

Working Hard

Get Lifted was released on Legend's twenty-sixth birthday, December 28, 2004. Legend celebrated the release with a free concert staged in a park in his hometown of Springfield. The concert also featured his family as performers. Fifteen members of his extended family had recorded "It Don't Have to Change" with John for his album. The song was a tribute to family and gospel.

Music critics immediately praised *Get Lifted* for its soulful sounds, which reflected Legend's church background combined with a touch of hip-hop. The song lyrics weren't old-fashioned, but their delivery did bring some comments about Legend being a new Stevie Wonder or Marvin Gaye.

"Ordinary People" became the hit. The ballad is about the everyday challenges of life for a couple. In a December 2004 interview with *Billboard*, Legend said about the song, "My parents were divorced for 12 years, and they got back together. The song shows that there are ups and downs in any relationship." Later, Legend's parents would split up again.

Tom Sinclair of *Entertainment Weekly*, who had reviewed *Get Lifted* two weeks after it was released, said he thought releasing "Ordinary People" as a single wouldn't happen. The

Legend and girlfriend Christine Teigen arrive at a Grammy Awards party in Beverly Hills, California, on February 10, 2008. Model Christy is of Thai and Norwegian descent but was born in Utah. The couple began dating in 2007.

song featured only John's singing and piano playing. Sinclair said that the simple production of the ballad was the opposite of the usual complicated arrangements and production found in modern rhythm and blues and hip-hop music. However, that simplicity turned out to be one of the song's strengths.

Commercial success built steadily, too. Within two weeks of the *Get Lifted* release, the album had climbed to number four on the charts, selling almost 200,000 copies. In February 2005, Legend began a 35-city tour, opening for Alicia Keys. He began his first headlining tour in June, performing in just as many cities.

Legend became known for his hardworking style in addition to his musical talents. In June 2007, he told Angus Batey, reporter for *The Guardian* (London), "It always amazes me that I should stand out among other artists for working hard. Shouldn't everybody work hard? . . . If you don't seize this opportunity, it's going to go away. You might not be as smart or you might not have as good a record, but there should be no excuse for not working hard."

There was one unwelcome side effect from all the singing that Legend did in 2005. His voice became strained, and his throat hurt. He consulted a voice coach for the first time. Total vocal rest was prescribed for a short time, and then John was coached into a smoother, cleaner tone. It was a change for him, as his voice had been described as raspy or raw, but his fans didn't seem to mind the new sound.

> *Within two weeks of the Get Lifted release, the album had climbed to number four on the charts, selling almost 200,000 copies.*

Legend was a headliner at the only North American stop for the 2008 THISDAY Africa Rising Music and Fashion Festival series. He performed at the Washington D.C., Kennedy Center on August 1. The Africa Rising Festival was started in Nigeria to show positive images of Africa through its music, fashion, and arts.

It was a great year for Legend, and the final months brought the news that he had been nominated for the eight Grammy Awards. After that success, it was clear that Legend was singing what people wanted to hear.

Legend reflected on the popularity of his music in a February 2006 interview with *The Washington Post*. "It's kind of crazy to me that so many people enjoy it. I can't really explain it. It's cool, but I'm already thinking about the next album and how much better I can make it."

Much of 2006 was devoted to writing the music and lyrics for his second album. Many artists worry that their second—or sophomore—album won't be as successful as the first. Legend knew that the secret to a successful sophomore release was to work hard at making it better than the first. He said of the new album, "I'm not going to put it out until I'm sure it's better than the last one. Everybody's got their timetables for when they want it to come out. I want it to come out this year, but it's going to come out when it comes out. It has to be ready. I have to love it."

> It (2005) was a great year for Legend, and the final months brought the news that he had been nominated for the eight Grammy Awards.

Legend wrote thirty songs in three months and selected thirteen for inclusion in his new album. Recording began for *Once Again* with the help of some famous producers, including will.i.am of the Black Eyed Peas and Kanye West. The new album wasn't quite like the first, so the question was how the fans would respond.

Show Me

Released in late October 2006, *Once Again* pleased his fans but puzzled some critics by the kinds of songs that Legend included. *Once Again* had his trademark ballads and some hip-hop-flavored songs, but there were also songs that might be called classic pop and even Brazilian bossa nova. Legend admitted to *Entertainment Weekly* that the album was "kind of all over the place, but it feels like it belongs together."

The first single was "Save Room," which was described as the kind of song Frank Sinatra might have sung many years ago. Music reviewer Tonya Jameson called it a combination of 1960s-era Motown soul and lounge music. Music programmers for radio stations were skeptical of putting it on their playlists because it was so different from the contemporary music being played on R&B/hip-hop stations.

While Legend might be concerned about whether his music gets radio play, he doesn't consider that more important than creating a song he likes. He said of "Save Room" in a December 2006 interview with Jameson, "It was different than everything else on the radio. I think it made the right statement. It showed I was willing to take some creative risks and commercial risk."

Once Again moved up the charts until it peaked at number three on *Billboard*'s album sales chart. Eventually it went platinum (meaning a million albums had sold), and then multiplatinum. In February 2007, Legend took home two more Grammy awards: one for Best R&B Vocal Performance—Male and one for Best R&B Vocal Performance by a Duo or Group ("Family Affair," performed with Sly and the Family Stone, Joss Stone, and Van Hunt).

In spring 2007, Legend toured with British singer/songwriter Corinne Bailey Rae, and later with Emily King. Concert venues were packed wherever he went. Although his love songs, like "Ordinary People," usually get the biggest audience response, he stirs his listeners with more topical songs, like "Coming Home," which is a wartime song that refers to the contemporary wars in Iraq and Afghanistan. John sings, "We pray we live to see another day in history. Yes, we still believe I'm coming/you know that I'll be coming home."

Another song became the vehicle for the 2007 launch of Legend's antipoverty work. Legend described to *LiveDaily* how his Show Me Campaign started. "It was kind of in response to a song that I wrote called 'Show Me' on the last album. The song is a prayer asking God why is there so much suffering in the world."

> *Once Again moved up the charts until it peaked at number three on Billboard's album sales chart.*

"Show Me" got John thinking about poverty and asking questions. He and his team answered those questions by coming up with a campaign to raise money for and awareness about the millions of people living in extreme poverty.

Legend performs with singer Estelle at the MOBO (Music of Black Origin) 2008 Awards in London on October 15, 2008. While working on the Show Me Campaign and producing his own music, Legend also signed her to his new HomeSchool Records label.

The Show Me Campaign partnered with Dr. Jeffrey Sachs and his Millennium Promise Alliance to help African villagers become more self-sufficient rather than just giving them money. The campaign provides mosquito nets to help stop the scourge of malaria, and free meals to children when they attend school. Safe water, medical clinics, and fertilizer for their crops are made available to the villagers through support from the Show Me Campaign.

Legend and his campaign have focused on Mbola, a village in Tanzania. He said of his team's efforts, "We decided we wanted to do something to at least save the lives of a few thousand of these people, so we started the campaign."

In early 2008, Legend began a series of appearances with Jeffrey Sachs at colleges across the country to challenge attendees to support the fight against poverty. He and Sachs answered questions about how students and others could get involved and make a difference in that fight. Legend sang at the end of each appearance.

At the opening event of the Poverty Action Tour at Columbia University, Legend told the crowd, "I don't want to be standing on the sidelines. I don't want to just show up at a concert once in a while and say something nice—I want to be involved."

It was clear to the college students that John Legend was doing what he said was impor-tant. His hands-on work with his African charity made him a role model to the students—who were only a few years younger than he was.

Mbola, Tanzania

Africa

New Gigs

*P*olitics were on Legend's mind, too, during winter 2008. The presidential campaign was in full gear, and Legend was a Barack Obama supporter. He joined other celebrities in recording a video supporting Obama. Will.i.am produced the video, called "Yes We Can," and released it on YouTube, where it received over 20 million hits within six months.

In late March, Legend previewed some of the tracks from his third album for *Entertainment Weekly* interviewer Margeaux Watson. There were several songs on which he collaborated with other artists and songwriters. He explained, "I'm not too proud to collaborate with somebody else that's really good. I'm trying to make the best album I can make."

Legend has always admired Martin Luther King Jr., and in April he appeared in a documentary honoring King's life. He sang a U2 song called "Pride (In the Name of Love)." Legend told WashingtonPost.com that he had read a lot about King when he was a child. When asked what he thought King's legacy was, he replied, "I think he's inspired really the whole country and the world. The themes and the ideas of his movement have inspired many other movements subsequently to achieve revolutionary things through nonviolence."

Legend testifies at a House Appropriations Committee special hearing on Funding For the Arts on April 1, 2008, in Washington, D.C. The hearing was one of the events for Arts Advocacy Day, when attention is called to the importance of art in U.S. schools and communities.

August brought an entirely new gig for Legend. He was chosen to sing at the Democratic National Convention in Denver, Colorado, where Obama would be named the Democratic presidential nominee. Legend sang a new song that he had written, "If You're Out There." He was accompanied by a choir as he sang, "We've been looking for the world to change. If you're out there, sing along with me. Stand up and say it loud. Tomorrow's starting now." The song echoed Barack Obama's campaign themes.

Earlier in August, Legend had made a trip to Tanzania, where he visited some of the villages that were benefiting from the Show Me Campaign. In Illongulu ward, he talked with farmers who proudly showed him the surplus maize that

Legend performs with James Taylor at the We Are One: The Obama Inaugural Celebration at the Lincoln Memorial in Washington, D.C. The concert was the kickoff for three days of events celebrating the inauguration of President Barack Obama. Unofficial estimates set the number of people braving the cold to attend the free concert at 400,000.

they had stored from their harvest. The record harvest was a result of the fertilizer and new seed varieties that the Show Me Campaign had funded.

The successful farmers would contribute a portion of their maize harvest to provide food for the meal program at Illongulu Primary School. Legend visited the school and saw the ample meals the children were fed. His next stop was the medical clinic, where villagers could obtain treatment for malaria and other diseases, as well as vaccinations. It was obvious that money raised by the Show Me Campaign was not going to waste.

Back in the states, Legend's third album, *Evolver*, was released on October 28, 2008. Once again he took a different direction. *Evolver* is more up-tempo and pop sounding than his first two albums. Steve Jones of *USA Today* called the first single, "Green Light," which featured rapper Andre 3000, "bouncy."

In an interview with *Billboard* magazine, Legend said, "This album doesn't sound like me. The tempo is faster than I've done before. It will be different for people, because *Evolver* has a bit more instrumentation than I've used before. But it's not like you won't recognize the artist — it's still me."

> *Legend visited the school and saw the ample meals the children were fed. . . . It was obvious that money raised by the Show Me Campaign was not going to waste.*

The following January, Legend was honored to be involved with the inauguration of Barack Obama as the 44th president of the United States. Legend performed at a pre-inauguration concert at the Lincoln Memorial. He wrote on his blog that the event was "pretty cool." He talked to many other

John Legend (back, right), fellow musician Wyclef Jean, and the African Children's Choir walk the red carpet to the OneXOne Foundation Gala in Toronto, Canada, on September 8, 2008. Legend performed at the children's charity benefit gala and was also honored for his work on behalf of African children through his Show Me Campaign.

stars backstage, but wrote, "No matter how famous the artists and athletes were, I think everyone was star-struck around the President-elect and his family. A few people even shed tears of joy. We all wanted photos and a handshake. A very memorable evening."

After the excitement of the inauguration, Legend headed back to work on the *Evolver* tour. He took a day off to perform during pregame festivities at Super Bowl XLIII.

Evolver was not eligible for the 2008 Grammy awards, but Legend was nominated for two featured roles, including Best Rap/Sung Collaboration for "Green Light" with Andre 3000. He won his sixth Grammy on February 8, 2009, for his performance with Al Green for Best R&B Performance by a Duo or Group with Vocals. The winning song was "Stay With Me (By the Sea)."

Legend was soon back on the road, singing and giving every bit of energy to his audiences. The *Evolver* tour took him from the United Arab Emirates to England, Sweden, and several other countries.

In a December interview with Craig Lindsey of the Raleigh, North Carolina, *News and Observer*, Legend explained how he wants his audience to react to his concerts. "You want them to love the music. You want them to feel inspired. You want them to feel connected, energized. I just want them to leave and say, 'That was the best show I've ever seen.'"

If the crowds at Legend's concerts are any indication, he is doing all that for his audience and more. And he plans to be making music for many years to come.

> *"I think everyone was star-struck around the President-elect and his family. A few people even shed tears of joy."*

CHRONOLOGY

1978	John Roger Stephens is born in Springfield, Ohio, on December 28.
1983	Begins piano lessons at age four.
1985	Attends Springfield Christian School after being homeschooled.
1990	After being homeschooled again for grades four through six, John is enrolled in eighth grade at Schaefer Middle School.
1995	Graduates second in his class from North High School in Springfield. Enrolls at University of Pennsylvania in Philadelphia. Joins the college a cappella group, Counterparts, and works as choir director for Bethel AME Church in Scranton, Pennsylvania.
1998	Makes major recording debut, playing piano on "Everything Is Everything," a track from *The Miseducation of Lauryn Hill*.
1999	Graduates from college and takes a job in New York City as a management consultant for Boston Consulting Group.
2000	Releases his first independent CD, *John Stephens*.
2001	Puts out another independent release, *Live at Jimmy's Uptown*.
2002	Plays piano and sings for Kanye West's debut album, *The College Dropout*.
2004	Is a featured performer on West's School Spirit tour. Takes stage name of John Legend. First major label album, *Get Lifted*, released December 28.
2005	Tours with Alicia Keys. *Get Lifted* is certified platinum. Single "Ordinary People" hits the top 40 and eventually is certified gold. Is nominated for eight Grammy awards.
2006	Wins Grammy awards for Best New Artist, Best R&B Album, and Best R&B Vocal Performance—Male. New album, *Once Again*, released in October.
2007	Wins two Grammy awards: Best R&B Vocal Performance—Male and Best R&B Vocal Performance by a Duo or Group ("Family Affair," performed With Sly & the Family Stone, Joss Stone, and Van Hunt). Launches his own record label, HomeSchool Records. Starts Show Me Campaign to raise money to fight poverty in Africa.
2008	Appears at colleges with Jeffrey Sachs to challenge students to join the fight against poverty. Supports Barack Obama in presidential race and joins other celebrities on video "Yes We Can." Sings "If You're Out There" at Democratic National Convention in August. Travels to Tanzania to visit villages funded by the Show Me

Campaign. Third album, *Evolver,* is released on October 28. Begins *Evolver* world tour in November.

2009   Performs at pre-inauguration concert at the Lincoln Memorial. Sings at Super Bowl XLIII pregame festivities. Wins sixth Grammy award for Best R&B Performance by a Duo or Group with Vocals, with Al Green for "Stay With Me (By the Sea)." Sings at half-time for the NBA All-Star Game.

DISCOGRAPHY

Albums
2008   *Evolver*
2006   *Once Again*
2004   *Get Lifted*

Soundtrack Contributions/Compilations
Independently Released
2003   *Solo Sessions Vol. 1: Live at the Knitting Factory*
2001   *Live at Jimmy's Uptown*
2000   *John Stephens*

Other Live Albums
2008   *John Legend: Live from Philadelphia*
2007   *John Legend: Live at the Tin Angel*
2006   *John Legend: Live at the House of Blues*

Novelty Album
2006   *John Legend: Sounds of the Season*

Singles
2009   "Everybody Knows"
2008   "Green Light"
         "If You're Out There"
2007   "P.D.A. (We Just Don't Care)"
         "Another Again"
         "Stereo"
         "Show Me"
2006   "Save Room"
         "Heaven"
2005   "Ordinary People"
         "Number One"
         "So High"
2004   "Used to Love You"

FURTHER READING

Books

Chang, Jeff. *Can't Stop Won't Stop: A History of the Hip-Hop Generation.* New York: Picador, 2005.

Gaye, Frankie. *Marvin Gaye, My Brother.* Milwaukee: Backbeat Books, 2003.

George, Nelson. *Where Did the Love Go?: The Rise and Fall of the Motown Sound.* Champaign: University of Illinois Press, 2007.

Ramone, Phil. *Making Records: The Scenes Behind the Music.* New York: Hyperion, 2007.

Reynolds, Andy. *The Tour Book: How to Get Your Music on the Road.* Swanton, Vermont: Artistpro, 2007.

Werner, Craig. *Higher Ground: Stevie Wonder, Aretha Franklin, Curtis Mayfield, and the Rise and Fall of American Soul.* New York: Three Rivers Press, 2005.

Works Consulted

Ali, Lorraine. "Living Legend." *Newsweek,* September 4, 2006.

"A Legend in Humanity." *The Washington Times,* June 18, 2008.

Batey, Angus. Interview with John Legend. *Guardian* (London), June 22, 2007.

"The Best New Artist Is Already a Legend." *The Washington Post,* February 9, 2006.

Christian, Margena. "John Legend Shifts Gears." *Jet,* December 15, 2008, Vol. 114, No. 22.

Conniff, Tamara, and David Greenwald. "Making of a Legend Part 2." *Billboard,* August 26, 2006, Vol. 118, Issue 34.

"Constantly Evolving Legend." *USA Today,* October 28, 2008.

Crosley, Hillary. "He's Got the Beat." *Billboard,* October 4, 2008, Vol. 120, Issue 40.

Edwards, Gavin. "Urban Legend." *Rolling Stone,* February 10, 2005, Issue 967.

Fuoco-Karasinski, Christina. "LiveDaily Interview: John Legend." *LiveDaily.com,* November 20, 2008. http://www.livedaily.com/news/15260.html. Accessed January 9, 2009.

Hall, Rashaun. "A 'Legend' Starts to Create His Own." *Billboard.* December 18, 2004, Vol. 116, Issue 51.

Jameson, Tonya. "Soul and Swagger: John Legend Speaks: Singer Says New Retro-flecked Album 'Makes the Right Statement.' " *The Charlotte Observer,* December 1, 2006.

"John Legend." *The Times* (United Kingdom). January 1, 2005.

"Legend in the Making?" *The Washington Times*, January 18, 2005.

"Legend Moves 'To the Next Level' to Build His Legacy." *USA Today*, October 23, 2006.

Lindsey, Craig. "A Legendary Sound: It's About More than Just Ballads." *The News & Observer*, Raleigh, North Carolina, December 12, 2008.

Odell, Jennifer. "John Legend Sounds Off." *People*, March 21, 2005, Vol. 63, Issue 11.

McGee, Tiffany. "5 Reasons Why John Legend Is No Ordinary Pop Star." *People*, November 6, 2006, Vol. 66, Issue 19.

Merrill-Moorings, Antracia. "John Legend Launches Own Version of 'Home School.' " *Frost Illustrated*, April 18, 2007.

"Remembering Martin Luther King Jr. with John Legend." *Washington-post.com*. April 4, 2008. http://www.washingtonpost.com/wp-dyn/content/discussion/2008/04/03/DI2008040301941.html. Accessed January 8, 2009.

Saunders, Tim. "A Legendary Evening in the Fight Against Poverty." *Look To the Stars; the World of Celebrity Giving.* January 21, 2008. http://www.looktothestars.org/news/529-a-legendary-evening-in-the-fight-against-poverty. Accessed January 8, 2009.

Scaggs, Austin. "Grammy Legend." *Rolling Stone*, March 9, 2006, Issue 995.

———. "John Legend." *Rolling Stone*, February 9, 2006, Issue 993.

Show Me Campaign. "Mbola, Tanzania." http://www.showmecampaign.org/ Accessed February 11, 2009.

Stone, Josh, "John Legend." *Interview*, August 2005, p. 100.

Thrills, Adrian. "I Want to Be a Pop Legend Now." *Daily Mail* (United Kingdom), October 10, 2008.

Watson, Margeaux. "John Legend." *Entertainment Weekly,* March 21, 2008.

Willoughby, Elizabeth. "John Legend Says 'Show Me.' " October 26, 2007. http://www.looktothestars.org/news/403-john-legend-says-show-me. Accessed January 8, 2009.

On the Internet

John Legend's Official Website
http://www.johnlegend.com

John Legend Network: The Official John Legend Fan Club
http://www.johnthelegend.ning.com

MTV: John Legend
http://www.mtv.com/music/artist/legend_john/artist.jhtml

INDEX